FASTING

VOLUME II

OPENING A DOOR TO GOD'S PROMISES

FASTING

VOLUME II

OPENING A DOOR TO GOD'S PROMISES

Jentezen Franklin

Published by Jentezen Franklin Ministries
Gainesville, GA.

FASTING VOLUME II
Opening A Door To God's Promises

Copyright© 2006 by Jentezen Franklin Ministries.

ISBN: 0-9759594-8-4

Published by Jentezen Franklin Ministries, Gainesville, GA.

For more information, contact:
Jentezen Franklin Ministries
P.O. Box 315
Gainesville, GA 30503
888.888.3473
www.JentezenFranklin.org

All Scripture quoted is taken from the King James Version of the Bible unless otherwise noted. Other Scripture quotations are from: The Holy Bible, New King James Version (NKJV), © 1984 by Thomas Nelson, Inc.

Scripture taken from the HOLY BIBLE NEW INTERNATIONAL VERSION®. Copyright © 1973, 1978, 1984 International Bible Society. Used by permission of Zondervan. All rights reserved.

Scripture taken from the Amplified® Bible, Copyright © 1954, 1958, 1962, 1964, 1965, 1987 by The Lockman Foundation. Used by permission. (www.lockman.org)

Cover & Interior Design: Roark Creative, *www.roarkcreative.com*

DEDICATION

This book is dedicated to all the members of our
Free Chapel and Kingdom Connection family who
faithfully join us in our First Fruits Fast each year.
We rejoice with you in all that God has done,
and will do as we seek Him together.

ACKNOWLEDGEMENTS

My sincere appreciation goes to Tomi Kaiser and the dedicated editors on my ministry staff. Your creativity and attention to detail are a blessing. Thank you for helping me utilize the printed page in order to reach more souls for the Kingdom of God.

TABLE OF CONTENTS

INTRODUCTION

When the woman saw that the fruit of the tree was good for food...
[Genesis 3:6 NIV]

It is still amazing to me that food was the enticement used to cause Adam and Eve to sin, resulting in the fall of all mankind. I find it equally interesting that Jesus began His earthly ministry—to redeem us from sin—by abstaining from food.

I imagine it was an extraordinary sight for John the Baptist to see his own cousin, the Lamb of God, descending into the water to be baptized like everyone else. Most of the folks who were baptized that day probably went home afterward to celebrate with a fine feast, talking about what they had seen and heard. Jesus did not. He followed the leading of the Holy Spirit, beginning His earthly ministry alone, fasting for forty days and nights while being tempted in the desert (see Matthew 3:16-4:11).

The first thing Jesus felt in His earthly ministry for you and me was hunger. The last thing that He felt on this earth was thirst as the Lord of Glory hung dying on a cruel cross, according to John 19:28.

So my question is: Why does the Body of Christ have such a hard time with the discipline of fasting? Lack of control over the flesh opened the door for sin's temptation in the Garden of Eden, but Jesus took control over His flesh, sanctifying Himself to break the power of temptation. When Jesus fasted for 40 days and nights, Satan tempted Him to "command that these stones be made into bread" (Matthew 4:3). The enemy tried repeatedly to cause Jesus to focus on the desire for food rather than on the assignment and the purposes of the Father, but Jesus knew that sanctification is an essential key to opening the door of God's blessings.

If Jesus needed to fast, how much greater is our need to fast? I was eighteen years old when I went on my first complete 21-day fast. It was one of the most difficult things I had ever done. Fasting is never easy. Honestly, I know of nothing more wearisome than fasting. Jesus understands the difficulty of depriving ourselves of food. In Hebrews 4:15 He says, *"For we do not have a High Priest who cannot sympathize with our weaknesses, but was in all points tempted as we are, yet without sin."* He also provides strength for us to overcome temptation in Hebrews 4:16. *"Let us therefore come boldly to the throne of grace that we may obtain mercy and find grace to help in time of need"* (NKJV). With these promises in mind, the process became less unpleasant for me.

When you fast, you abstain from food for spiritual purposes. I have heard people say that they were planning to fast TV, or computer games, or surfing the Internet. It is good to put those things down if they are interfering with your prayer life, or with your study of God's Word, or your ministering to the needs of others, but technically, that is not fasting. Fasting is doing without food for a period of time, which generally causes you to leave the commotion of normal activity. Part of the sacrifice of fasting, seeking God and studying His Word is that normal activity fades into the background.

There are wrong reasons to fast. You do not fast to obtain merit with God, or to get rid of sin. There is only one thing that gives us merit with God, and cleanses us of sin—the Blood of Jesus. However, fasting will begin to bring to the surface any areas of compromise in your life and make you more aware of any sin in your own life so you can repent.

Fasting is not a Christian diet. You should not fast to lose weight, although weight loss is a normal side effect. Unless you put prayer with your fasting, there is no need to fast. Merely doing without food is just starving. When you fast, you focus on prayer and on God's Word.

Finally, you do not fast so that others will notice you. A fast is not an opportunity to show others how deeply spiritual you are, but an opportunity to focus on the needs of others. The World Hunger Movement has a program called "Let It Growl," in which teenagers participate in a thirty-hour fast. During that time, when they feel the hunger pangs rise up and their stomachs begin to growl, they remember that one-third of the people in this world go to bed with that same feeling every night because they have no food.

At the time of this writing, I have been pastoring Free Chapel for just over sixteen years. For much of that time, I fasted privately for 21 days at the beginning of each year, but about five years ago, the Holy Spirit led me to ask the church to join the fast. God has blessed us in more ways than I could have ever imagined.

I was walking through the airport the other day and a man stopped me and said, "I know who you are. I am one of those people who fasted with your church last year." When you enter into a fast at the beginning of the year with the Body of Christ, you link up with thousands of people all over the world who also begin the New Year with a fast. One person fasting is powerful, but when a group of people begin to fast, it is multiplied strength! It is multiplied power!

Dr. Cho pastors the largest church in the world in Seoul, Korea. Seven hundred and fifty thousand members go on a 21-day fast every year. He has fifteen hundred teenagers camp out on Prayer Mountain in tents to fast and pray for seven days each year.

You have been deceived if you believe Christians are not supposed to fast. God expects every one of us to fast, not just some of us. In Matthew chapter 6, He names three things that Christians do: *"When you pray ... When you give ...And When you fast."* He didn't say "if" but "when." If you have a time to pray, and you have a time to give, then you should have a time to fast.

"Therefore do not worry, saying, 'What shall we eat?' or 'What shall we drink?' or 'What shall we wear?' ... For your heavenly Father knows that you need all these things. But seek first the kingdom of God and His righteousness, and all these things shall be added to you." (Matthew 6:31-33 NKJV)

You can always find a reason not to fast, so you have to make up your mind that you are going to do it, and everything else will take care of itself. If you will determine to set apart the first days of the year to fast, you will set the course for the entire coming year, and God will add blessings to your life all year long. Just as you set the course of your day by meeting with God in the first hours, the same is true of dedicating the first days of the year to fasting.

I titled my first book, *Fasting: The Private Discipline That Brings Public Reward*. The "rewards" that have surfaced in the lives of those attending Free Chapel and beyond over the past few years have been phenomenal. In this second volume, I will share some of the deeper teachings the Lord has given me on fasting as we have continued to seek Him in this manner, and I will encourage you with some of the magnificent testimonies of God's faithfulness to His Word.

Jentezen Franklin

CHAPTER 1

HE PLEASED GOD

And all these, having obtained

a good testimony through faith,

did not receive the promise,

God having provided something

better for us, that they should not

be made perfect apart from us.

—[HEBREWS 11:39-40 NKJV]

I am more excited about fasting than I have ever been. Don't get me wrong—*I enjoy eating!* Though, I enjoy eating, I cannot say I enjoy watching people as they cut into a big, steaming, juicy steak while I'm crunching on steamed broccoli, I have found that hungering and thirsting for God brings with it a much greater reward than satisfying the temporary hunger I may be experiencing in my body.

Do you remember Anna? Her story only fills a few lines in Luke's Gospel, but I believe God saw much more in the life of this precious saint. She is called a prophetess, and her simple testimony is that she was *"a widow of about eighty-four years [of age], who did not depart from the temple, but served God with fastings and prayers night and day"* (Luke 2:37 NKJV). That just goes to show you that you are never too old to fast. Anna had a hunger for God's Word that was greater than her hunger for food, and her faithfulness in fasting prepared her for what was about to happen.

> HUNGERING FOR GOD BRINGS WITH IT A MUCH GREATER REWARD THAN SATISFYING THE TEMPORARY HUNGER IN MY BODY.

After Jesus' birth, Joseph and Mary brought their tiny infant boy to the Temple to be dedicated as the first-born Son.

I would imagine that young family walked past hundreds of people in the crowded Temple that day, but only one man and one faithful woman truly recognized the Messiah. Simeon was the first to rejoice in seeing Jesus. Then Anna saw Him and instantly gave thanks to God. She then began telling all who looked for the redemption of Israel about the tiny Baby who was the long awaited Messiah (see Luke 2:38). Imagine that—a new calling on her life at 84-years old!

WHEN THE HOLY SPIRIT CALLS YOU TO FAST, HE IS PREPARING YOU FOR WHAT IS AHEAD.

Although fasting doesn't get any easier with age...it does get easier with grace. When the Holy Spirit calls you to fast, He is preparing you for what is ahead. Fasting requires faith. As Jesus said, *"Blessed are they which do hunger and thirst after righteousness: for they shall be filled"* (Matthew 5:6).

GOD IS

The eleventh chapter of the book of Hebrews is often referred to as "the hall of faith," beginning with the words, *"Now faith is the substance of things hoped for, the evidence of things not seen"* (Hebrews 11:1 NKJV). Some of the most encouraging words in the Bible are found in this book. It is said that, after the birth of Seth to Adam and Eve, people began to call on the Name of the Lord (see Genesis 4:26). Enoch was born many years later, and his life went a step beyond merely calling on the Name of the Lord. Thousands of years after his departure from this earth, the writer of the book of Hebrews said of him: *"By faith Enoch was translated that he should not see death; and he was not found, because God had translated him: for before his translation he had this testimony, that he pleased God"* (Hebrews 11:5).

What was it about Enoch that was different from those before him? What about his life was so pleasing to God? The answer is found in verse 6 of Hebrews 11:

"But without faith it is impossible to please Him: For he that cometh to God must believe that He is, and that He is a rewarder of them that diligently seek Him."

Enoch knew God. Not only that, Genesis 5:22 says that Enoch *"walked with God"* for three hundred years! Now, if I were to choose what could be said of me, I would want my testimony to be "he pleased God." Notice that Enoch did not try to please people. In fact, Jude records that Enoch prophesied in a manner that would have made him very unpopular with the party crowd (see Jude 14-15). Enoch's primary concern was walking in faith, which is what pleases

God. According to Hebrews 11:6, it is reasonable to say that Enoch came to God...he believed God...he diligently sought God...and he was rewarded.

If you want to please God...*believe* God. Take Him at His Word. When the Apostle Paul was teaching the Corinthians, a very knowledge-seeking society, he told them, *"We walk by faith, not by sight"* (2 Corinthians 5:7). Shadrach, Meshach and Abed-nego walked by faith and not sight. The three of them joined Daniel in his initial fast from the King's delicacies. Think about what they saw on their way into that furnace. It had been heated seven times hotter than normal. The heat was so intense that it killed the guards standing by the doors. If they had walked by sight, they would have said, "Today we shall surely be ashes." Instead, by faith they walked on saying, *"Our God whom we serve is able to deliver us from the burning fiery furnace, and He will deliver us from your hand, O King"* (Daniel 3:17 NKJV). Faith is the evidence of things "unseen."

HUNGER FOR THE WORD

Faith which enables you to look to God and believe His Word, no matter how grave your circumstances may *appear*; where does such faith come from? Your daughter is unsaved and on drugs...Your father lies dying in a hospital bed...You are about to be evicted from the house you rent because it's been sold out from under you...Your marriage of 20+ years has come to an end and the divorce papers have been signed. I could go on and on. These are very real circumstances that have no solution in the natural. Where does such faith come from?

"Faith cometh by hearing, and hearing by the word of God" (Romans 10:17). The Amplified version of this scripture states, *"Faith comes by hearing [what is told], and what is heard comes by the preaching [of the message that came from the lips] of Christ (the Messiah Himself)."* It is by hearing God's Word, by hearing the preaching of the Gospel, that faith increases. There is something about getting in a church where the anointing flows and you hear the Word of God preached. Faith does not come from programs, dynamite worship teams or being with a group of people who are like you. Faith comes when you hear a man or woman of God preach the Word without compromise to all who will listen. That is the birthplace of faith. If this revelation truly takes hold of your spirit, you will never allow the devil to talk you out of being faithful to God's House.

IF YOU WANT TO PLEASE GOD... BELIEVE GOD.

Too many Christians find that they are malnourished in

the Word, but well fed on the world; and they live defeated lives as a result. In the Introduction, I mentioned how Eve *saw* that the fruit was good for food. God's Word to Adam and Eve was, "Do not eat of it or you will surely die" (see Genesis 2:17). Yet Eve acted on the wisdom of the world that was spoken by the serpent instead of walking away in faith that God's Word was true.

In contrast, as Jesus fasted in the desert, He was tempted by the same voice that had so cunningly whispered to Eve. Yet Jesus responded, *"Man shall not live by bread alone, but by every word that proceedeth out of the mouth of God"* (Matthew 4:4). What had Jesus heard just before beginning that time of fasting? *"And lo a voice from heaven, saying, 'This is my beloved Son, in Whom I am well pleased'"* (Matthew 3:17). The Word of God sustained Him through forty days and nights without food.

How I wish the Body of Christ today had that same kind of hunger for God's Word. I would love to see the day when, if a Christian had to, he or she would go to church in pajamas rather than miss *hearing* God's Word! I know that sounds extreme, but we live in extreme times. We need to understand Jesus' words when He said, *"Heaven and earth will pass away, but My words will by no means pass away"* (Mark 13:31 NKJV).

In the natural, what did young David possess that

made him believe he would be successful against the giant Philistine? Nothing! He was small, he was young, he was not yet a soldier—merely a keeper of sheep. Yet, he walked with God, he knew God and he sought after God. His faith was all he needed to know that Goliath would fall before him just as the lion and bear had fallen.

DILIGENCE!

We must diligently feed on God's Word. Sometimes the best thing we can possibly do is to starve our flesh and feed our spirit through a fast. Fasting helps you separate what you *want*...from what you *need*. It causes you to focus on those things that really matter.

Believe me, fasting allows you many opportunities to "diligently seek the Lord!" You can diligently seek Him when everyone is going out to the movies, drinking sodas, eating popcorn, but you choose to stay home to be with the Lord because you just _have to_ hear from Him. Diligently seeking Him through fasting happens in the morning when everyone else gets up and eats bacon, eggs, pancakes, real maple syrup, grits, hash browns, fried sausage...and there you sit with some raw nuts and a sliced orange. It comes when you're at work and everyone else is having burgers, fries and shakes for lunch, but you are having broccoli and bottled water! Diligence is when you come home from a long, hard day at work, and all you have had all day is water, yet you separate yourself from the dinner table to feed on the Word.

To be diligent is to be persistent. It means to work hard in doing something and refusing to stop. God delivered the Israelites from Pharaoh's slavery. He parted the Red Sea so they could cross on dry ground, but allowed Pharaoh's army to drown. Yet, they got out into the wilderness and started complaining. After all He had done for them, still they were not diligent about seeking the Lord, and that older generation never entered into His rest...His reward.

WE WALK BY FAITH, WE DON'T STAY STILL, DROWNING IN OUR MISERY.

Faith is progressive. Faith never gets into a bad situation and says, "I'm just going to sit here and die, it's over." Faith never stands in the desert having a pity party with everything drying up around it. We walk by faith, we don't stand still, drowning in our misery. When you get in a wilderness, you keep walking; you keep going forward even if you are only making an inch of progress with each step. When you get into battles you have to keep saying, "I will move forward."

REWARD

When a reward is offered for someone's capture, the reward is provided before it is claimed. The money is placed into an account to be held until the offender is captured. God is a rewarder of those who diligently seek Him, which means He has already laid up rewards for you in Heaven. In my mind, when reading this scripture I've always added, "seek Him.... *and find Him.*" That is not what it says. The Bible tells us that if we *seek, we will* find.

Free Chapel begins each year with a season of fasting and praying—*seeking* first His kingdom. The testimonies that come during and after the fast are incredible. I want to share some of their "rewards" to encourage you in your faith. Often during the services in January, the microphone will be overrun with people testifying to the goodness of God. I will let some of them share with you in their own words...

"I have been fasting for my family and my children to get saved and I've gone seven days with no food, just liquids. I was trying to decide whether to start on the Daniel Fast today or not. Well, I'm not going to do that because after two years of running from the Lord, my daughter got saved this very morning—and I want more miracles in my family!"

⌒

"Pastor, we were behind on our house payment, facing foreclosure. Friday, my company bought pizza for everybody. I sat in my office and ate tomato soup instead. I got home that afternoon to discover that the bank had rearranged the whole mortgage. We're caught up! We're current! And don't have a payment until the first of April!"

⌒

"We've been praying for my daughter-in-law for a year and a half. She has recently gone into a drug program from church. She's been on drugs since she was fourteen. She was up here at the altar this morning on her face crying out to God. It's a miracle. It is a miracle!"

⌒

"I've been attending Free Chapel for three years, but last year my mother told me, "They're starting a fast." I thought, "Twenty-one days, I don't know if I can do that." Then I remembered that, when you put God first the year will be prosperous. At that time my wife and I had just one car and we were living in an apartment. Over the course of the year, I got another car. We moved into a house. I'm a musician, and the artist I have worked with just got a deal with one of the biggest labels in the world. So my family and I will be on the fast again this year—and who knows!"

⸱⸱⸱

"My father is in CCU at Northeast Georgia Medical Center. He had a hernia that had enclosed his colon, which basically killed the colon, the bowel and everything. Five times he has been given up for dead. Right now he is off the vital life support. He is breathing on his own. And they're talking about moving him to a room."

⸱⸱⸱

"Pastor, this week we had a major mess up in our bank account. Some people had stolen our card, debit card, and some money and we started bouncing checks. But Praise God, we started fasting. You know, God just came down! We got all the money back for the bounced checks and they reimbursed the money that was stolen from us too."

⸱⸱⸱

I want to share this one with you myself. One year, at the end of the 21-day first of the year fast, a couple walked up to me and handed me a bundle of official looking papers. Puzzled, I opened them up to see the words "DISMISSED" stamped in bold black letters. After that I read the words, "The Superior Court of Gwinnett County, State of Georgia, Final Judgment and Decree of Divorce." The couple standing before me had been struggling in their marriage for a year, but during that fast, the season of setting everything else aside and diligently seeking God, a miracle happened! Unity replaced division, and the divorce was dismissed. The devil thought he'd racked up another statistic for Christian divorces—but God is a Rewarder!

The enemy comes *"to steal, kill and destroy,"* but Jesus came that we might have *"life more abundant"* (see John 10:10). There are many things that Jesus' death, burial and resurrection provide for us. While all are available, none are automatic. God is no respecter of persons. He rewards all who diligently seek Him, in faith believing, because faith is what pleases Him.

CHAPTER 2

GARMEN† OF PRAISE

I will lift up my eyes to the hills—

From whence comes my help?

My help comes from the LORD,

Who made heaven and earth.

He will not let your foot slip—

He who watches over you will not slumber;

Indeed, he who watches over Israel

Will neither slumber nor sleep.

—[Psalm 121:1-4 NKJV]

Y̶ou never forget the feeling of sorrow and loss that occurs when someone close to you dies. I loved my father dearly. When he passed away in 1991, it took me weeks to get beyond the initial impact of grief and mourning. Each day when I awoke, that sense of loss would hit me again as I thought, "My daddy is dead." He was a wonderful father and grandfather. I am thankful that we had the opportunity to make so many wonderful memories together. His life was indeed a celebration. Though I knew Dad was with the Lord, his absence from this life left a void that took a while to get over.

> ❧
>
> YOU WILL HAVE
> TO CHOOSE
> TO DETHRONE
> THAT "DICTATOR
> WITHIN"!

In Matthew 9:14-15, we see the disciples of John the Baptist coming to Jesus to ask

"Why do we and the Pharisees fast often, but Your disciples do not fast?"

Jesus answered, *"Can the friends of the bridegroom mourn as long as the bridegroom is with them? But the days will come when the bridegroom will be taken away from them, and then they will fast."* (NKJV)

This is not the only time you see the words "mourn" and "fast" used interchangeably in the Bible. The example the Lord gives in this passage makes it clear that fasting is much like mourning. When you are on a fast, you usually do not feel like celebrating. It is a time to press into God, to seek Him and to forsake the things of the flesh. Within hours of beginning a fast, you may find that food is the first thing on your mind (right before your stomach begins to growl).

Still, I look forward to the corporate fast here at Free Chapel each year because of the rewards that come from the diligence of an entire church seeking God in that manner. Jesus said, *"Blessed are they that mourn: for they shall be comforted"* (Matthew 5:4). Who is the Comforter other than the Holy Spirit? As the prophet Isaiah began his proclamation of the Good News in Chapter 61, he foretold of the coming of Christ, who came to

> ...*Comfort all who mourn,*
> *To console those who mourn in Zion,*
> *To give them beauty for ashes,*
> *The oil of joy for mourning,*
> *The garment of praise for the spirit of heaviness;*
> *That they may be called trees of righteousness,*
> *The planting of the LORD, that He may be glorified.*

I believe that as the Church learns to fast (mourn) together, we will see God begin to fulfill these promises in many ways. Are there "burnt out" experiences in your life—ugly reminders of past hurts and failed dreams? Don't throw away the ashes. God will give you beauty for ashes. He will give you the anointing of His presence which is the oil of joy for your mourning.

FASTING BREAKS THE SPIRIT OF HEAVINESS

The "spirit of heaviness" has to do with despondency, depression and oppression. Sadly, the biggest pitfall in America is the oldest in the world. Americans use drinking, smoking, drugs, medications, overeating and other harmful behaviors to try and lift the spirit of heaviness. Think about all the commercials you see for weight loss, stop-smoking cures, anti-depressants, etc. Seldom do you turn on a television program without being bombarded by drug company commercials.

Instead of looking for more stuff to put *into* our bodies to ease the pain, we should fast and seek the God who gives us a garment of praise for the spirit of heaviness that afflicts so many. Why is it a garment of praise? You will find that you wear depression and oppression like a garment. It shrouds you in darkness and despair. It is a heavy garment that continues to drag you down. It keeps you from lifting your head and from raising your hands in praise to God.

Heaviness drains worship out of your life. Church is depressing unless you learn to worship. I know that is a strange statement, but it is true. There is nothing worse than a Spirit-filled church that loses "the garment of praise" and picks up "the spirit of heaviness." God desires our praise more than our mere church attendance. That is not to say we should forsake assembling together as a corporate body. But our times together, just as our times alone, should be to glorify and praise our awesome, mighty God. Praise pushes back the enemy!

One of my favorite examples of this fact is found in 2 Chronicles 20. King Jehoshaphat is told *"a great multitude is coming against you from beyond the sea, from Syria; and they are in Hazazon Tamar (which is En Gedi). And Jehoshaphat feared, and set himself to seek the Lord, and proclaimed a fast throughout all Judah"* (vs 2-4 NKJV).

Now, Jehoshaphat had just gotten the kingdom of Judah in order. Things were going well. No sooner did they start enjoying that peace before they heard that an army—far larger than they could defeat on their own—was already on its way. Jehoshaphat could have taken that spirit of heaviness and died under it. The scripture says *"he feared,"* but he only paused a moment there. He immediately set himself, and all the people of Judah, to seek the Lord through fasting and prayer. Then he took his place in the assembly of the people and began to praise—proclaiming who God was and all that God had done for them. He ended saying, *"...We have no power against this great multitude that is coming against us; nor do we know what to do, but our eyes are upon You"* (vs 12 NKJV). Then they waited.

How many times do we find ourselves saying that same thing: "I don't know what to do. This problem is far too big for me to handle." We must put our eyes on God! The story continues: *"Then the Spirit of the LORD came upon Jahziel... a Levite of the sons of Asaph, in the midst of the assembly."* God told them that the battle was not theirs but His. He told them exactly where the enemy would be, but said, *"You will not need to fight in this battle. Position yourselves, stand still and see the salvation of the LORD, who is with you, O Judah and Jerusalem!' Do not fear or be dismayed; tomorrow go out against them, for the LORD is with you"* (vs 14-17 NKJV).

I don't know about you, but realizing that the Lord was going to destroy my enemies would be reason enough to shout! And that is just what the people of Judah did. Young and old *"stood up to praise the Lord God of Israel with voices loud and high."* The next day, they went early to the place the Lord had directed them. Then Jehoshaphat addressed the people again saying,

THERE IS POWER IN CORPORATE FASTING AND POWER IN CORPORATE PRAISE!

"Hear me, O Judah and you inhabitants of Jerusalem: Believe in the LORD your God, and you shall be established; believe His prophets, and you shall prosper." And when he had consulted with the people, he appointed those who should sing to the LORD, and who should praise the beauty of holiness, as they went out before the army and were saying: Praise the LORD, For His mercy endures forever." (vs 20-21 NKJV)

Now, notice what happened when they began to praise: *"The LORD set ambushes against the people of Ammon, Moab, and Mount Seir, who had come against Judah; and they were defeated"* (vs 22 NKJV).

There is power in corporate fasting and power in corporate praise! It creates a river of healing...a river of deliverance and victory...a river of cleansing in the house of

God. It is time to exchange ashes for beauty, mourning for joy, and heaviness for praise.

What Eating Accomplishes

A friend called me just as we were about to begin the corporate fast. To my surprise he said, "I feel so sorry for you." He actually felt sorry for me because I was about to lay down food for the joy of seeking the Lord for 21 days.

I replied, "Don't feel sorry for me. In fact, I feel sorry for you." Then I challenged him: "I'll make a deal with you. Go ahead and eat your food for the next 21 days. We will compare notes at the end of the year to see if the food you ate accomplished for you what fasting for the next 21 days accomplished for me." As evidenced in Daniel 1:15, eating does not accomplish what fasting does.

I am so blessed to be part of a fellowship that seeks God together through fasting. Battles are won and lives are changed as a result of fasting. In fact, a dramatic change came around Christmastime in the life of a young man who I will call James. We had started that year off with a corporate fast, as we now do every year. Many miracles had occurred in the lives of people throughout the year. This particular Friday night, my family and I had attended the Christmas program at Free Chapel and were driving home. The forecast was calling for severe winter weather to hit our area over the weekend, so my wife asked me to stop by the grocery store to pick up some essentials. It was late, so I pulled up right out front and left the car running to keep them warm.

I grabbed the milk, bread and cereal, and got in line at the checkout. I could see my kids watching me through the store windows. That's when I noticed him. A young man had entered the store right behind me, and was now in line behind me holding a few cases of beer. I glanced back at him, and our eyes met for a second. At first, I didn't think much about it because I was just there to get milk and cereal. Remember, I had fasted for 21 days at the beginning of the year and fasting makes you more sensitive to the voice of God. Suddenly, in my spirit I heard the Lord say, *"Tell him he has great worth to Me."*

I looked back at the young man, and he looked at me, and then he walked away. I went through the line and paid for my things, knowing I was supposed to say something to him. I didn't see him as I left, so I walked out to the car. When I opened the door, Cherise and all the girls were saying, "Daddy, Daddy, look, look, look." They showed me the camera they had brought to take pictures of the

Christmas drama. But when I looked at the digital screen, they had taken pictures of the guy from the line. I asked, "What's going on?"

My wife and kids had a birds-eye view of this guy stealing beer and wine from the store. Not only that, they took pictures of him in the act! That's right, the same young man of whom God said, "He has great worth to Me." My heart sank. I had the chance to tell this young man that he had great worth to God, that he didn't have to continue living like he was living, defeated by the enemy and trapped under a spirit of heaviness. I had not obeyed God and I felt terrible.

I confessed to my family, "The Lord spoke to my heart but I didn't obey Him." I jumped out of the car and I went back into the store. I looked frantically for the guy in the aisles, and one of my girls ran up behind me and said, "Daddy, he went out the other door." My heart sank again. When I walked outside and got in my car, Cherise said, "I know where he went. He went to the next supermarket down the street."

I said, "You think so?"

She said, "I guarantee you he did. He's in a red Camaro."

I said, "Let's go." Thank God for second chances!

We rode down to the next supermarket and as we

cruised through the parking lot one of the girls said, "There it is! It's the red Camaro!" I immediately parked, jumped out of the car, and ran inside to look for him. I knew just where to look: the beer and wine section! There he was, with the cart filled to the top with cases of beer and wine. He had pushed it to the edge of the aisle where he could slip out behind the cash registers and ease on outside with his load.

But that wasn't God's plan for James! I walked right up to him and I said, "You don't know me and I don't know you, but God wants you to know that you have great worth to Him." He stared at me for a moment and said, "What did you say?" I reached in my pocket and I had forty dollars. Handing it to him I said, "I know when I give you this money you're probably going to buy that alcohol with it, but I've got to obey God and He told me to tell you sir, "You have great worth to Him and He loves you."

He said, "I can't believe this is happening. Who are you?"

I said, "I'm a Preacher."

"Where do you preach?"

"At Free Chapel over on McEver Road."

He started to tremble and said, "Thank you... I can't, you know, I can't quit," pointing to the cart. He said, "I've been in six rehabs and I can't quit."

Again I told him what God said about him. He backed up a step or two. I asked, "Are you ready to walk out of here and leave it?" He looked at me very seriously and said, "Let's go!" We walked to the parking lot. Now, the girls are all sitting in the car praying for this guy the whole time that I'm talking to him. The guy walks out wiping tears from his eyes. I put my arm around him and said, "You just need to ask Jesus to help you, son. He knows. He understands. He sent me during this Christmas Season to tell you, 'You have great worth.'"

Everyone else, including James himself, had said "You're worthless...You'll never amount to anything...You're a failure...You've wasted your life..." But God saw things differently. I prayed with James in that parking lot, and we parted ways. The last thing he told me was, "I'll be at your church, pastor." I began to pray for him every day. Christmas came and went. New Year's came and went. We were a few days into our corporate fast when I saw him walking toward me one Sunday morning. It was James, with a big smile on his face. He said, "I told you I'd be here." We started our year off with a miracle!

No matter what is going on in your life right now, you can set yourself to fasting and praying to seek the God who sees you as having great worth. Don't believe the lies of the enemy. Don't sink further under the spirit of heaviness. God has a garment of praise for you. His yoke is easy and His burden light. As you fast, you begin to see yourself through His eyes.

CHAPTER 3

FASTING, FAITH & PATIENCE

That you may walk worthy of the Lord, fully pleasing Him, being

fruitful in every good work and increasing in the knowledge

of God; strengthened with all might, according to His glorious

power, for all patience and long-suffering with joy, giving thanks

to the Father who has qualified us to be partakers

of the inheritance of the saints in the light.

—[Colossians 1:9-11 NKJV]

I don't really remember what grade I was in, but we did an experiment in elementary school that left a lasting impression on me, even into adulthood. The teacher told us to save our milk cartons from lunch for this special event. We were to bring them back to class with us, where we rinsed them out and cut the funny tops off. She then opened a big container of black potting soil and we scooped some into our cartons. She handed each one of us a big butter-bean seed and told us how to plant the seed in the soil by making a small hole with our finger and dropping the seed in. After I pressed the dirt back down into the hole, I watered the seed, taped my name to the box, and set it in the sunny window beside everyone else's.

Everyday when that class started, I ran to the window with the others to see what was happening with the seeds. We couldn't see anything until the third day, when a tiny bit of green sprout began to show in some of the boxes. By day six, most of the boxes had green sprouts, and some even had leaves showing—but not mine. For six days I eagerly ran to the window to look at my box; there was nothing but dirt. I watered it like everyone else did. It sat in the same sun that everyone else's did, but no sprout was showing. I wondered if my seed was even still there.

On the seventh day, I couldn't take it any longer. I arrived to class before anyone else, and used my finger to dig around in the soil to see if my seed was still in the box. I pulled it out, and sure enough, it had begun to sprout. My teacher walked in about that time. When she saw what I had in my dirty little fingers, she kindly explained that I really should have left it alone and just waited. Since I had pulled my seed out of the soil too soon, I had destroyed my harvest. She was right. All the other seeds grew strong and tall, and before long, they were filled with multiple pods of butter beans—far more than the one seed that was sown.

Don't Dig it Up!

That little childhood experiment has stayed with me for so long because I have learned that we do the same thing in our spiritual lives. We get a word from the Lord—it's just a seed—but it gets planted deep in our hearts: "God is going to bless me...I'm highly favored of the Lord...God sees my need and will provide for me...He will protect my family and save my lost loved ones..." The mountains you face seem so big, but you take that tiny seed of faith and plant it into that mountain, and wait.

But before long, impatience sets in. The mountains seem even bigger than they were before, and your seed isn't showing any sprouts—no matter what you do. Other people are being blessed, but nothing is happening in your situation. You begin to think, "Did I really get that word from God?" Like my wondering if my seed was still in the little box; I knew I had planted it and I didn't think anyone had taken it—but surely it must be gone because I couldn't see anything. You end up getting discouraged. You dig your fingers in and pull your seed out too early, destroying the promise.

Likewise, I've heard people say they just couldn't make it past a day or so on a fast because they got discouraged. They listened to their flesh instead of continuing in faith and felt worse than when they started. What happened to walking by faith and not by sight? Faith and *patience* must go together.

FAITH AND PATIENCE GO TOGETHER.

When a man brought his son to the disciples to deliver him from seizures, the disciples were not able to help him. So he brought the boy to Jesus, asking the Lord to have mercy on his son. Jesus cast out the demon that tormented the boy and he was healed. I can imagine how the disciples began to question themselves, and each other. Later, they asked Jesus why they could not cast it out. Jesus answered them saying,

"Because you have so little faith. I tell you the truth, if you have faith as small as a mustard seed, you can say to this mountain, 'Move from here to there' and it will move. Nothing will be impossible for you." (Matthew 17:20 NIV)

What powerful words Jesus gave us. I encourage you to meditate on this scripture for a while, and not just pass over it as familiar territory. People facing major obstacles usually believe they need "great faith" to overcome them, but that isn't what Jesus said. He said "nothing" would be impossible to us—not if we had *great faith*—but if we had faith like the smallest seed.

Someone once sent me a mustard seed, I believe from Israel. Just to put things into perspective, a butter bean seed is about 400 times bigger than a mustard seed, but it will yield only a small bush. On the other hand, a common mustard seed is only about one millimeter in diameter, and it grows into a small tree. The more common mustard plants are perennial, growing back year after year and developing deeper root systems each season. You could try to pull one of these little trees out of the ground, but the stems would most likely break, leaving the roots to regenerate a new plant.

That is the type of faith we are to have! Jesus put the

emphasis on how great our God is...not how great our faith is. With only a tiny bit of faith, like a mustard seed, we can move mountains and nothing shall be impossible.

As Christians, we need to stop measuring our faith by the size of the problem. We need to start looking instead at how great our God is. We need to plant that seed of faith—no matter how small—into whatever mountain stands in our way and believe it will be moved, because Jesus said it would.

When Peter tried to walk on water, he made it only a few steps because he took his eyes off of Jesus and fear dragged him down.

> **WE NEED TO STOP MEASURING OUR FAITH BY THE SIZE OF THE PROBLEM.**

When he began to sink, Jesus lifted him up out of the water and said, "Ye of little faith." Peter did have a little faith because that is what it took to walk on water.

If he could do that with just a little faith, imagine what will happen when that faith increases!

REMEMBER THE FAITH

In the closing chapter of the book of Hebrews, the writer tells us, *"Remember your leaders, who spoke the Word of God to you. Consider the outcome of their lives and imitate their faith"* (Hebrews 13:7 NIV). As I asked before, if our Lord fasted, why would we think that we should not fast? There is no record of Jesus ever healing anyone until He returned from the forty days of fasting that launched His earthly ministry. Jesus said we would do even greater works than He had done, because He was returning to the Father. If Jesus did not begin to minister before fasting, how can we?

Throughout the history of the Christian church, God has raised up men and women who were willing to dedicate their lives to Him, and diligently seek Him through fasting and prayer. Long seasons of fasting are credited for launching such revivals as seen by Evan Roberts in Laos, who fasted and prayed for thirteen months for that country. Healing evangelists like John Alexander Dowie, John G. Lake, Maria Wordworth-Etter, Smith Wigglesworth and Kathryn Kuhlman all understood the tremendous power of faith in operation throughout their ministries.

NOT GETTING THROUGH?

There may be times when you are fasting and praying, and standing in faith, yet you still do not sense that anything is happening. There's no "sprout" showing through the dirt.

Remember the faith of those before you. David said, *"I humbled myself with fasting; And my prayer would return to my own heart. I paced about as though he were my friend or brother; I bowed down heavily, as one who mourns for his mother"* (Psalm 35:13-14 NKJV).

Do not let the enemy drag you down with discouragement. Remember, God gives you the garment of praise for the spirit of heaviness. Sometimes you will not feel like praying when you are fasting, but pray anyway. You will be amazed how God will show up, and it will be like all of heaven has come down and glory has filled your soul.

†THE LORD WILL REWARD YOUR DILIGENCE

In this same Psalm, David had not yet received an answer to his prayer, yet he is able to wait in faith, proclaiming the praises of God: *"Let the LORD be magnified, who has pleasure in the prosperity of His servant. And my tongue shall speak of Your righteousness and of Your praise all the day long"* (Psalm 35:27-28 NKJV). The Lord will reward your diligence; His delight is in the prosperity—the wholeness—of His children.

Remember the faith of Abraham, *"the substance of things hoped for, the evidence of things not seen"* (Hebrews 1:1 NKJV). It was that faith which was accredited to him as righteousness—because he *believed* God. Even though Abraham's body was dead as far as fathering children was concerned, he still desired a child of his own. God desired it even more and gave him the promise of not only a son, but descendants more numerous than the stars of the sky (see Genesis 15:4-6). When you believe Him for some*thing*, you are exercising faith, which pleases God. Are you dreaming the dreams of God for your life and your family? Are you believing Him for those *things*—those evidences—to come to pass?

CHAPTER 4

GOD'S PRIORITIES

Now He who searches the hearts knows
what the mind of the Spirit is, because He
makes intercession for the saints according to
the will of God. And we know that all things work
together for good to those who love God, to
those who are the called according to His purpose.

—[Romans 8:27-28 NKJV]

It seems unnecessary to begin this chapter by pointing out how God's priorities are seldom our priorities. That is the difference in the nature of man, and the nature of God. He even said so: *"As the Heavens are higher than the earth, so are my ways higher than your ways and my thoughts than your thoughts"* (Isaiah 55:9 NIV). So, how do we position ourselves to hear from God? How do we free ourselves from our own desires, to know His Will? Well, I can tell you from first-hand experience that fasting causes you to take that sword of God's Word, and separate what you "want" from what you "need."

THERE IS NO HIGHER AUTHORITY THAN TO KNOW THE HEART OF GOD FOR A SITUATION YOU ARE FACING.

"Let us therefore be diligent to enter that rest, lest anyone fall according to the same example of disobedience. For the word of God is living and powerful, and sharper than any two-edged sword, piercing even to the division of soul and spirit, and of joints and marrow, and is a discerner of the thoughts and intents of the heart. And there is no creature hidden from His sight, but all things are naked and open to the eyes of Him to whom we must give account." (Hebrews 4:11-13 NKJV)

There is that word "diligent" again. Fasting, prayer and

feeding on the Word of God puts that sword in your hand, and positions you to discern the difference between your thoughts and God's thoughts. There is no higher authority than to know the heart of God for a situation you are facing. His Word is final!

GET IN LINE

Imagine living just doors away from where Jesus lived much of His earthly ministry and never getting swept up into His message or miracles. Cornelius is such a man. He must have been a rather busy man, because he completely and totally missed the move of God. Luke tells his story in the book of Acts. He begins, *"There was a certain man in Caesarea called Cornelius, a centurion of what was called the Italian Regiment, a devout man and one who feared God with all his household, who gave alms generously to the people, and prayed to God always"* (Acts 10:1-2 NKJV).

So we know that this generous, probably kind-hearted Italian man had been around the Jewish faith enough to begin to believe in their God, and to pray to Him, but as yet, the Gospel of salvation through the Blood of Jesus was a message that had only come to the Jews, not to the Gentiles. Still, Cornelius was diligent—and his diligence is why those of us who are not of Jewish descent are able to call upon the Name of the Lord and be saved today.

The Bible tells us that around the ninth hour of the day, an angel appeared to Cornelius, and told him to send for Peter in Joppa, and listen to what Peter would tell him. So he faithfully sent his most trusted men to Joppa to bring Peter back with them. Now, stop here and think a moment. Here's a man who is not born again, but is devoted to God. Was he just walking around his house, watching a game on TV when this angel appeared to him? Not hardly.

When Peter arrived at his house, Cornelius said, *"Four days ago I was fasting until this hour; and at the ninth hour I prayed in my house, and behold, a man stood before me in bright clothing, and said, 'Cornelius, your prayer has been heard, and your alms are remembered in the sight of God'"* (Acts 30-31 NKJV).

Cornelius was fasting and praying. He was diligently seeking God when that angel came to tell him that his diligence was about to be greatly rewarded. Peter preached the Gospel to them, and "While Peter was still speaking these words, the Holy Spirit fell upon all those who heard the word. And those of the circumcision who believed were astonished, as many as came with Peter, because the gift of the Holy Spirit had been poured out on the Gentiles also.

For they heard them speak with tongues and magnify God"
(Acts 10:44-46 NKJV).

Those of us who are not of Jewish descent can thank
one man for being diligent to seek the Lord and bring the
message of the Cross to the Gentiles. Cornelius gave to the
poor and he prayed often, but he was a lost man. Fasting puts
you in the main stream of God's priorities.

God established priorities as early as the book of Genesis.
His principle of first things is stated clearly in Exodus 13
verses 11 and 12:

*"And it shall be, when the LORD brings you into the land of
the Canaanites, as He swore to you and your fathers, and gives
it to you, that you shall set apart to the LORD all that open the
womb, that is, every firstborn that comes
from an animal which you have; the males
shall be the LORD's."* (NKJV)

**FASTING PUTS
YOU IN THE MAIN
STREAM OF GOD'S
PRIORITIES.**

This is an amazing text to me.
Throughout Scripture, God makes it clear
that the firsts—firstlings of flocks, first
fruits of harvest, first-born males of flocks and families—all
belong to Him. The Old Testament is full of types and shadows
of things revealed in the New Testament; namely that Jesus
is the first-born Son. Two thousand years ago, that spotless

Lamb redeemed those of us who were made unclean by sin when he offered His own Blood on the altar in Heaven.

GO VERTICAL

For ten years and 230 episodes, the TV sitcom, "Friends," became a focal point for millions in this country. In 1994, the critics said this show about six 20 to 30 something single friends living in New York City was not very entertaining, clever or original. The final episode of that show had 52 million viewers. The critics who said it wouldn't make it didn't take into account the great vacuum for connection in American culture. People want and need to be connected in relationship.

That need to be connected is evidenced in the Church by home groups and a greater emphasis on community. While that is good, if we're not careful we can become too horizontally focused and not enough vertically focused. Church right now, for the most part in the Western world, particularly in America, is all about *me*; "I want my needs met...bless me...teach me...help me..." While those are legitimate needs and desires, we must keep in mind that the cross has two beams: one is horizontal—but the other is vertical.

Fasting turns your priorities more vertical...more in line

with God's desires. It's what Jesus did when He cleared the temple. They had become excessively "horizontal."

"Then Jesus went into the temple of God and drove out all those who bought and sold in the temple, and overturned the tables of the money changers and the seats of those who sold doves. And He said to them, "It is written, 'My house shall be called a house of prayer,' but you have made it a 'den of thieves.'" (Matthew 21:12-13 NKJV)

That doesn't mean that when you fast, you don't have specific needs and desires of your own for which you are seeking God. Indeed you should fast for a specific purpose. However, I believe that as you continue on a prolonged fast, the true cry of your heart becomes: "More of You God, and less of me." When you put Him first, all else is added.

THE ORDER OF THINGS

I want to show you several key aspects of life that we tend to get out of order. First, we often miss the significance of Paul's words in 1 Thessalonians 5:23, *"Now may the God of peace Himself sanctify you completely; and may your whole spirit, soul, and body be preserved blameless at the coming of our Lord Jesus Christ"* (NKJV). Notice that God's priority is concern for your spirit first...your soul second...and your body third.

We get that totally backwards, always focusing on our bodies first, and our spirits last. We worry about "What will I wear?" ... "What will I eat?" ... "Where do I need Botox?" Jesus told us not to worry about such things, saying, *"Is not life more than food and the body more than clothing?"* (Matthew 6:25 NKJV).

According to God's principle of "first things," what you put first will order the rest. When you put your spirit first, you serve the things of the Holy Spirit rather than the desires of the flesh. As a result, your mind, will, emotions, as well as your physical body and health will fall in line according to the Spirit's leading. *"For if you live according to the flesh you will die; but if by the Spirit you put to death the deeds of the body, you will live"* (Romans 8:13 NKJV).

WHAT YOU PUT FIRST WILL ORDER THE REST.

...FORGIVENESS

Another area that too frequently becomes out of order has to do with reconciliation and public worship. Notice what is to be "first" according to Jesus: *"If you bring your gift to the altar, and there remember that your brother has something against you, leave your gift there before the altar, and go your way. First be reconciled to your brother, and then come and offer your gift"* (Matthew 5:23 NKJV). First be reconciled. God desires our public and corporate worship. However, those public acts of worship do not fix our private acts of strife, contention and unforgiveness.

I heard a story once about a local woman who moved back to Georgia to purchase the old homestead on which she'd grown up. Her mother and father had passed away, and the land had to be claimed. One of the first things she had to do was hire some one to come clean out the well that her father had dug many years before. Over the years, a lot of stuff had accumulated in the well, and made the water worthless. The crew got a good-sized pile out and showed the woman so they could get paid for the job. But she said, "Nope. There's more in there. Please keep digging." This went on for about three days. Finally, at the end of the third day, the woman looked at the latest pile of trash, toys and miscellaneous objects that had found their home at the bottom of the well and said, "You're done." Puzzled, one of the men asked how she knew that was it. She answered, "Because when I was a little girl and Papa first dug that well, I took a teapot and threw it in the well. I figured the first thing that went into that well would be the last thing that came out."

Fasting allows the Holy Spirit to come in and, just like those well diggers, He can begin to dig up stuff that needs to come out of your spirit. You will have a hard time accepting the grace and forgiveness of the Lord, if you haven't gotten down to that "teapot" in your own heart. You have to get out that first offense you stored up years ago, and sometimes, you will have to dig for a long time. But then that river of living water can spring back up out of you and refresh others. That is God's priority.

DIRTY CUPS

What else does the Lord expect us to keep first? In the words of Jesus, *"Woe to you, scribes and Pharisees, hypocrites! For you cleanse the outside of the cup and dish, but inside they are full of extortion and self-indulgence. Blind Pharisee, first cleanse the inside of the cup and dish, that the outside of them may be clean also"* (Matthew 23:25-26 NKJV). Jesus was teaching the people to obey the laws of God taught by the Pharisees, but instructed the crowd not to do as the Pharisees. They had gone overboard into legalism, and in their extremes, had gotten things out of order. For example, they cleaned a pretty cup on the outside, but the inside was still full of crud that they had not cleaned out. Whether you are talking about your life, or your cup, first clean the inside, because that makes all the rest much more presentable. Fasting will cause you to get the crud out, cleaning the inside, which will then make the outside clean.

SOMETHING IN YOUR EYE?

Another "first" is found in Matthew 7:1-5:

"Judge not, that you be not judged. For with what judgment you judge, you will be judged; and with the measure you use, it will be measured back to you. And why do you look at the speck in your brother's eye, but do not consider the plank in your own eye? Or how can you say to your brother, 'Let me remove the speck from your eye;' and look, a plank is in your own eye? Hypocrite! First remove the plank from your own eye, and then you will see clearly to remove the speck from your brother's eye." (NKJV)

Before you will be ready to perceive wrong in someone else's life, you first need to do a little self-examination of your own. You're worried about a tiny splinter in their eye, when you have a telephone pole in your own. Hypocrisy is judging somebody else when there is something worse going on in you. Our attitude and lifestyle should be as Paul directed the church in Galatia:

"Brethren, if a man is overtaken in any trespass, you who are

spiritual restore such a one in a spirit of gentleness, considering yourself lest you also be tempted. Bear one another's burdens, and so fulfill the law of Christ. For if anyone thinks himself to be something, when he is nothing, he deceives himself." (Galatians 6:1-3 NKJV)

The word "restore" used here comes from a Greek medical term meaning to re-set, like one would set a shoulder that's out of joint. Sometimes we need to remember that someone may be out of joint, but they are not out of the Body. When saints get out of joint, they need tender hands. They need trained hands to reset and restore them.

...KINGDOM FIRST

I've touched on this briefly, but this is another area that Christians tend to get out of order. Jesus said, *"So do not worry, saying, 'What shall we eat?' or 'What shall we drink?' or 'What shall we wear?' For the pagans run after all these things, and your heavenly Father knows that you need them. But seek first his kingdom and his righteousness, and all these things will be given to you as well"* (Matthew 6:31-33 NIV). Again, fasting helps you distinguish between what you want and what you really need. When you choose not to worry about these things and to seek Him first, you are demonstrating the kind of faith that is pleasing to God, because you are trusting Him to also give you all the things that you need.

If poverty has killed its thousands, prosperity has killed its tens of thousands. We all need to heed the warning of Jesus: *"Take heed to yourselves, lest at any time your hearts be overcharged with surfeiting [overindulgence], and drunkenness, and the cares of this life..."* (Luke 21:34).

...First Love

What would your answer be if the Lord were to ask, "Do you remember the last time you were lovesick for Me?" I began to ponder that question recently. I thought back to the time when Cherise and I were dating. We were deeply in love and wanted to spend every moment together. It was probably a good thing our parents wouldn't let us because we would have surely starved to death. For the longest time, whenever we would go out to eat, we would end up taking about three bites because we were so engrossed with each other. I know that sounds a little sappy, but stay with me—I have a point. I cannot tell you the money I wasted on meals, simply because we desired to talk and spend time with each other more than our desire for food. We were "lovesick" for each other. As I thought back on that, it hit me. That is what the Lord feels when we fast. When we are so lovesick for our First Love, fasting is easy.

So I ask you, do you remember the last time you walked away from a meal because you were so preoccupied with your First Love that the food was of no interest? Have you experienced seasons when it felt like the Bridegroom was distant? You just don't sense His presence as close as you once did. You have no heart for worship and you lack the excitement and child-like enthusiasm

DO YOU REMEMBER THE LAST TIME YOU WERE LOVESICK FOR GOD?

you once had for spiritual things? Perhaps it is time to stop the busyness of your everyday life and declare a fast, a season of lovesickness to restore the passion of your First Love back to its proper place in your life. When you fast everything slows down. The days seem longer. The nights seem longer, but in the quietness of seeking, you will find Him whom your heart desires.

CHAPTER 5

FOR THE LITTLE ONES

Walk about Zion, And go all around her.

Count her towers; Mark well her bulwarks;

Consider her palaces; That you may tell it

to the generation following. For this is God,

Our God forever and ever; He will be

our guide Even to death.

—[Psalm 48:12-14 NKJV]

There is another very important priority on God's agenda, and for this one, I needed an entire chapter. God sees far beyond what our limited minds can comprehend. For the most part, whenever we hear Joshua's words, *"As for me and my house, we will serve the Lord"* (Joshua 24:15), we think of our spouses, our children, maybe even our grandchildren. God sees *generations*.

In the more recent corporate fasts at Free Chapel, the Lord has laid on my heart this passage from Ezra 8:21-24:

"Then I proclaimed a fast there, at the river of Ahava, that we might afflict ourselves before our God, to seek of him a right way for us, and for our little ones, and for all our substance. For I was ashamed to require of the king a band of soldiers and horsemen to help us against the enemy in the way: because we had spoken unto the king, saying, The hand of our God is upon all them for good that seek him; but his power and his wrath is against all them that forsake him. So we fasted and besought our God for this: and he was intreated of us."

After seventy years of Babylonian captivity, Ezra was about to lead the remnant of Israel back to the Holy Land— an entire generation of young people who had never seen the Temple of Jerusalem, including some very small children. It was going to be a treacherous journey home, but they had boasted in God's mighty hand of protection *before* heading out, so they had to act in faith and *believe* their own words. Settled by the river, Ezra proclaimed a fast so that the people might humble themselves before God and seek His face. They needed to know the right way they should take, for their protection and for their "little ones."

We fast because we need to know the "right way" for our lives. We do not need to be confused as to our future or the choices before us. Fast, seek His face and have faith that He will guide you. "Should you take that new job? ... Should you marry her? ... Should you marry him?" It is biblical to fast and seek God for the right direction in your life. Examples are found in Judges 20:26 (Israel seeking to know if they should go into battle against the tribe of Benjamin), 1 Samuel 7:6 (seeking God at Mizpah for forgiveness and protection against the Philistine army) and 2 Chronicles 20:3 (Jehoshaphat inquiring about the army about to attack).

> WE FAST BECAUSE WE NEED TO KNOW THE "RIGHT WAY" FOR OUR LIVES.

We also fast...for our little ones. I had not noticed the tenderness in that language before. Usually it is assumed that there were children in the midst of the pilgrims. But here, Ezra sees such promise, such potential and such grave danger for the next generation. It was tempting to request an army to go with them. Perhaps Ezra remembered an old song of David, one that went something like,

I know that the LORD saves his anointed; he answers him from his holy heaven with the saving power of his right hand.

Some trust in chariots and some in horses, but we trust in the name of the LORD our God.

They are brought to their knees and fall, but we rise up and stand firm. (Psalm 20:6-8 NIV)

A few verses later, we see that God heard, and answered their prayers. Fasting with praying just seems to open a different frequency in God's ear! Ezra recorded that they left the river Ahava after twelve days to set out for Jerusalem. He also testified, *"The hand of our God was on us, and he protected us from enemies and bandits along the way"* (vs 31 NIV). God's hand was upon them, His right hand protecting them...and their little ones!

THE UNBLUSHABLES

Today, if we have lost anything in this country, we have lost the "right way." Yet I ask you: Who is fasting for the protection of our little ones in this age?

Today, fasting has all but disappeared from regular Christian discipline. We have more media availability for preaching than ever before, yet sin and repentance are seldom preached.

Today, our little ones are exposed to every kind of perversion and danger with a click of a button—be it TV, Internet, cell phones—or just a stroll through the local mall.

Today, the words of the weeping prophet Jeremiah cause a lump in my throat as I read them aloud. Speaking of a sinful generation the Lord said,

"Are they ashamed of their loathsome conduct? No, they have no shame at all; they do not even know how to blush. So they will fall among the fallen; they will be brought down when I punish them." (Jeremiah 6:15 NIV)

In an age where gay and lesbian experimentation is considered normal on campuses today...when oral sex and every type of perversion imaginable is just winked at (kids call that "technical virginity" now)...when sexual affairs before and after marriage are totally acceptable...our little ones are positioned to be an unblushable generation. Already they are becoming so familiar with sin that when they see immodest filth, they giggle when they should blush and turn away instead.

A popular news show has begun exposing men who solicit sex over the Internet.

Why is that so newsworthy?

The men are soliciting the vilest acts from children whose ages are 12, 13 and 14. They drive to the home of the child, and walk in even bringing alcohol or entering the home already stripped naked. Sadly, when confronted by a reporter who is waiting inside the house, few of these men even show embarrassment or remorse over their disgraceful actions. One man actually showed up with his 4-year old son.

There is an enemy that is taking captive entire generations in America today. Its grip is getting tighter and tighter—reaching farther and farther. We are standing at the crossroads. *"Stand at the crossroads and look; ask for the ancient paths, ask where the good way is, and walk in it, and you will find rest for your souls"* (Jeremiah 6:16 NIV).

OUR ONLY BOAST IS IN OUR GOD!

We have the opportunity to stand up like Ezra, to declare a holy fast for our children (Ezra 8:21), and to seek the Lord for the "right way" to lead this generation through. Since we have been fasting at Free Chapel, we are already seeing God's hand leading them through. My oldest daughter, Courtney, completed the full 21-day fast this year. She is a junior in high school and has become very aware of her own salvation and of the times in which we live. I believe as a result of the fast, she came to me recently with urgency in her heart and said: "Daddy, I love God, but I still don't know what His plan is for me. I don't know who I am and I don't know what God wants me to do."

We need to learn to trust the reliability of Scripture when things get crazy. God's promises are your "gauges" when the

WE NEED TO LEARN TO TRUST THE RELIABILITY OF SCRIPTURE WHEN THINGS GET CRAZY.

storm of life rages. A man in our church is a pilot, and he sometimes lets me fly with him. He has taught me a few things about flying. The most crucial thing is to train yourself to rely on what the gauges in the plane tell you. When you fly a small plane into a storm, that plane is bounced in every direction and you cannot rely on what you feel. Your equilibrium gets out of balance and you won't know if you're flying right side up. The only thing that will take you safely through is relying on the gauges—relying on the Scriptures.

It is humbling to shut off your mind to what worldly wisdom and insight says is "right," and yield your trust to a few digital gauges on an airplane dashboard, but there's a lesson in that. James said:

"God opposes the proud but gives grace to the humble. Submit yourselves, then, to God. Resist the devil, and he will flee from you. Come near to God and he will come near to you. Wash your hands, you sinners, and purify your hearts, you double-minded. Grieve, mourn and wail. Change your laughter to mourning and your joy to gloom. Humble yourselves before the Lord, and he will lift you up." (James 4:6-10 NIV)

Daniel humbled himself before the Lord. He fasted and prayed for three weeks, and an angel came to him and said, *"Do not be afraid, Daniel. Since the first day that you set your mind to gain understanding and to humble yourself before your God, your words were heard, and I have come in response to them"* (Daniel 10:12 NIV).

I want you to understand, you are not "twisting God's arm" when you go on a fast. You are not going to make God do anything He does not want to do. What you are actually doing is positioning yourself and preparing your heart for what is to come. He is not unwilling to give, if you are willing to seek Him.

Any time you fast, it is a hunger-strike against hell. Fasting is an extreme "in your face" statement to the Devil—that same Deceiver who used food to tempt Adam and Eve to sin. Gandhi was a humble Indian leader who went up against the British Empire for the freedom of his nation. He didn't fight them with violence. He would simply go on a hunger strike and the attention of the world was drawn to his plight.

When we fast, we are effectively going on a hunger strike against hell to say "Loose those who are bound by deception, lies, alcohol, drugs, pornography, false religion, etc!"

ANYTIME YOU FAST, IT IS A HUNGER-STRIKE AGAINST HELL.

One Sunday morning as I arrived at Free Chapel, a faithful woman from our congregation met me at the door. She had been fasting for 21 days and had a wonderful report. She began,

"My husband and I made it a matter of prayer during the fast to focus on the unsaved people in our family. I have two nieces who are sixteen and fourteen, and a sixty-year-old brother—all are practicing Buddhists. My sixteen-year-old niece has accepted Jesus as her Savior, and about ten days into the fast, my fourteen-year-old niece got saved. Not only that, but I was talking to my brother yesterday and he told me that he accepted Jesus as his Savior, which is a miracle!"

Another lady shared this testimony with the congregation:

"I guess about six weeks ago I gave you my children's names and asked you to pray for them because none of them were saved. My oldest is twenty-six, I have a twenty-year old, one eighteen and one thirteen. My twenty-six year old decided two weeks later that he was going to move to Texas and live with my sister and her husband because he had a job offer just out of the blue.

After you counseled with me about this, Pastor, I decided just to hand it over to the Lord no matter what happened. After he got to Texas he called me and said, 'Mom, Aunt Angela (my sister) said that if I was to stay here with them and live with them that I was going to have get up and go to church with them every Sunday.'

I turned the phone away and said, 'Hallelujah!' I told him, 'Then go, son.' He said, 'Okay.' Their church is a small, Bible-believing Church. He started going with them and called me a week later. He asked, 'Mom, are you coming down for Christmas?' I said, 'Yes, I'm coming to see you.'

He said, 'Would you get me a Bible for Christmas?' And I said, 'Okay...what does that mean?' My son answered, 'Mom, I've been saved!'

Something you need to know is, since my divorce, my oldest son has been a strong male figure in my home. All the other kids really look up to him, and with his salvation, they've been calling him about things, and just confiding in him about things that they *wouldn't tell me. So, I really feel like my other children are going to come to the Lord before this year is out."*

~

A woman from San Antonio wrote to tell us:

"My sister, nephew and I joined you and your church in the 21-day fast this year for the first time. I am seeing the hand of God over me and my family. Things are changing, moving like never before. I saw my son sober and in his right mind for the first time in many years (he is 35). God Bless you and you church for being obedient to the Lord."

~

This next story was shared by a precious couple that is on staff with us at Free Chapel. The husband says:

"While we were still dating, my wife's doctor told her that she would probably never bear children because of some issues that medication was not reversing. Her physician gave a low chance of things ever improving.

Shortly after getting married, we moved to Gainesville and were on staff with Free Chapel when we first heard the 21-day fasting message by Pastor Franklin. His message encouraged everyone to believe for 4 rewards during the fast, one of which was a physical healing. Every morning, we would take communion and pray the fasting focus. On the 21st and final day of the fast, there was a celebration service where we would all break our fast together. My wife had been feeling tired and just for the sake of it, took a pregnancy test. Sure enough, she was pregnant!

We joke that we weren't trying or even asking for signs and wonders, but God delivered a wonderful confirmation of our faith on the final day of our sacrifice to Him. Suddenly, there was this womb that doctors said would never exist. Our OB would joke with every monthly visit, being a Christian himself and knowing our story, that here was another by-the-book check up; perfect measurements, perfect weight gain. What's more, my wife was never sick during her pregnancy and never had any complications. Caden became so comfortable that he was actually a week late.

After five pushes and a half-hour of delivery, a healthy 8-pound 5-ounce baby boy was born. Caden has been in the 95 percentile for his weight and height since being born, and all of this from a 5' 2" mother who only weighs 105 pounds dripping wet. Our son has yet to be sick, break a bone or end up in the hospital for an earache, etc. Caden was also born on my birth date, a pretty cool coincidence, and will turn 4 this October 2nd."

It is time for parents to stand up like Ezra and fast, seeking God for His right way and for His protection over this generation. Our little ones are waiting.

CHAPTER 6

IS YOUR BLADE SHARP ENOUGH?

For the word of God is living and powerful,

and sharper than any two-edged sword,

piercing even to the division of soul and spirit,

and of joints and marrow, and is a discerner of

the thoughts and intents of the heart.

—[Hebrews 4:12 NKJV]

Can you imagine having an extended conversation with, not just any angel, but one of the higher-ranking angels of God? Suppose that angel came to you and told you of kingdoms that would rise and fall in coming years, even explaining what principalities would manipulate those leaders and how alliances would form and be crushed as new kings rose to power. I'd be willing to give up a Twinkie or a T-bone steak for a few weeks in order to have my spirit open enough to receive such a visitation!

Of course, I'm talking about Daniel, the faithful man of God who was held captive in Babylon for most of his life. After Nebuchadnezzar besieged Jerusalem and took captives back to Babylon, he had the best and brightest of the young men set apart. They were to be trained for three years in the ways of the Chaldeans, to eventually become his personal assistants. Daniel was among those selected, along with his three friends whom we have come to know by their Babylonian names: Shadrach, Meshach and Abed-nego. Early on, Daniel and his friends set themselves apart from the others by refusing to defile themselves with the foods laid out for them from the king's table.

Notice that by simply taking such a stand, *"God granted Daniel favor in the sight of the commander of the officials"* (Daniel

1:9 NASB). Daniel explained that he and his friends would be in better shape after ten days by eating only vegetables and drinking only water, than the others would be after eating the King's delicacies. The overseer continued giving them only their requested vegetables and water, and *"God gave them knowledge and intelligence in every branch of literature and wisdom; Daniel even understood all kinds of visions and dreams"* (Daniel 1:17 NASB).

Daniel rose to positions of great responsibility within the kingdom of Babylon, even under subsequent rulers. In chapter ten, Daniel, then close to 90 years old, received a message of great conflict and a vision, both of which he understood. Apparently troubled, he recorded, *"In those days I, Daniel, was mourning three full weeks. I ate no pleasant food, no meat or wine came into my mouth..."* (Daniel 10:2-3 NKJV). The Hebrew word used here for "pleasant food" is lechem, or breads. So for 21 days, Daniel fasted all sweets, breads and meats, and only drank water.

IT IS TIME WE SET OURSELVES APART TO SEEK THE LORD AND FIND UNDERSTANDING.

It was soon after that fast when Daniel's encounter with the angel of God took place along the Tigris River. Notice something very encouraging in what the angel told Daniel: His prayers had been heard in heaven from the very first day he started the fast (see vs 12)! The only reason the angel had not appeared to Daniel sooner was because he was fighting with the principality of Persia (modern-day Iraq).

DULL BUT COMFORTABLE

Of the many different types of fasts that are acceptable, what has come to be called the "Daniel Fast" is probably one of the more common—and with good reason. It is one of the personal fasts recorded in the Bible that brought with it great favor from the Lord. For 21 days, you eat only vegetables and fruits, and drink only water. No colas, burgers, Twinkies— no meats, sweets, breads, etc.

In the times in which we now live, when the enemy is taking our youth captive to sin at an alarming rate, when acts of Iraqi terrorism claim hundreds of lives and perversion is at an all-time high, like Daniel—it is time we set ourselves apart to seek the Lord and find understanding. Paul said,

"Finally, be strong in the Lord and in his mighty power. Put on the full armor of God so that you can take your stand against the devil's schemes. For our struggle is not against flesh and blood, but against the rulers, against the authorities, against the

powers of this dark world and against the spiritual forces of evil in the heavenly realms. Therefore put on the full armor of God, so that when the day of evil comes, you may be able to stand your ground, and after you have done everything, to stand. Stand firm then, with the belt of truth buckled around your waist, with the breastplate of righteousness in place, and with your feet fitted with the readiness that comes from the gospel of peace. In addition to all this, take up the shield of faith, with which you can extinguish all the flaming arrows of the evil one. Take the helmet of salvation and the sword of the Spirit, which is the word of God." (Ephesians 6:10-17 NKJV)

Have you ever seen a military man try to fit into his uniform 30 years later? Usually, it won't even come close to buttoning down the front. When you're a soldier, you stay fit, you stay healthy, alert and ready. Paul said we should live that way because the days are evil. The enemy prowls around waiting to attack. Just as the angel told Daniel, principalities of nations rise up to do battle, but we live as retired military, growing fat and comfortable.

Moses fasted. Elijah fasted forty days. Paul fasted fourteen days. Jesus fasted forty days. If the children of God do not fast, how will we ever fit into the armor of God? How will we effectively wield the sword of the Spirit?

I want you to understand something: Fasting and prayer sharpen the blade, which is the Word of God. When you fast, mealtimes often become study times. You become more keyed-in to God's Word, and God begins to show you deeper truths. It wasn't after finishing off a bag of chocolate-covered donuts that Daniel got the visit from the angel. Daniel began to understand God's truths after fasting and getting alone with Him. Understanding comes from the study of God's Word!

Many Christians have just stopped fighting all together because they are battered and bruised or using dull blades to fight demonic powers. When you fast and pray, you effectively sharpen the Word in your mouth. Instead of flippantly quoting scripture, you now wield a powerful weapon with a razor-sharp edge that slashes the enemy when you speak.

Amazing isn't it? Simply by missing some meals and setting your heart on understanding by studying God's Word, you please God, you release beauty for ashes, joy for mourning and the garment

WHEN YOU FAST AND PRAY, YOU SHARPEN THE WORD OF GOD IN YOUR MOUTH.

of praise defeats the spirit of heaviness. Your praise goes forth and scatters the enemy, you develop patience, you come in line with God's priorities, you loose angelic messengers, and you find God's right way for you and protection for your little ones. When are we going to take dominion back from "king stomach" and seek diligently after the Kingdom of God in this way?

AMERICA LIKE NINEVEH

America has greatly sinned against God through abortion, homosexuality, adultery, rampant pornography and fornication. We have no fear of God and America is rapidly becoming a pagan nation. Our only hope is to humble ourselves in fasting and prayer.

Nineveh was a great city. In fact, the Bible states that it was so vast it took three days just to tour it. Historians say Nineveh had walls 100 feet high with watchtowers that stretched another 100 feet. The walls were so thick that chariots could race on top of them. Surrounding the city of about 120,000 people was a vast moat 150 feet wide and 60 feet deep. Nineveh was proud, strong, and impregnable. And if any foreign army wanted to lay siege or attempted to surround and cut them off, they had enough supplies to hold out for at least 20 years. But Nineveh was a sin-filled nation.

I want to stop there a moment and point something out. I'm sure not all the people of Nineveh were sinning. There were children and probably plenty of common, decent, God-fearing people, but remember what happened in the battle of Ai? Joshua and the people of Israel had just defeated Jericho. Yet one man took the holy things that were devoted to God and hid them amongst his own belongings. When Joshua sought the Lord after that crushing blow from such a tiny city, God said, *"Israel has sinned"* (Joshua 7:11). Only one man took the devoted things, but he brought sin on the entire camp. He was stoned along with his wife and children.

Daniel's fast and visitation from the angel is recorded in Daniel chapter ten. Throughout chapter nine, Daniel cries out to the Lord on behalf of all Israel saying over and over, "We have sinned and done wrong...We have been wicked and rebelled...We have sinned against you..." Daniel identified with the sin of his nation, though we see no sin that Daniel himself had committed.

God sent Jonah to preach repentance to Nineveh. He proclaimed, "Forty more days and Nineveh will be overturned." It is very possible that the people of Nineveh had some understanding of how powerful the God of Israel was, because they were struck with fear at these words and believed them. They declared a fast and the king even issued a decree that no man or animal was to taste food or even water.

Without any guarantee, he thought by humbling themselves in this manner, God may *"relent and with compassion turn from his fierce anger so that we will not perish"* (Jonah 3:9 NKJV).

God did turn from His anger and spared the city, but they again ceased to seek the Lord. About a hundred years later, the prophet Nahum prophesied judgment on that city, *"The LORD has given a command concerning you, Nineveh: 'You will have no descendants to bear your name. I will destroy the carved images and cast idols that are in the temple of your gods. I will prepare your grave, for you are vile'"* (Nahum 1:14 NIV).

America has had its times and seasons. America started out as a faith-filled, God-fearing nation—pledging allegiance to our country with the words, "One Nation, Under God, Indivisible..." We chose to imprint our coins and money with the words "In God We Trust," in order to set ourselves apart as a nation that honored God with our finances and our lives. Many a fiery evangelist has brought the message of repentance to our nation: Charles Finney, Dwight L. Moody, Jonathan Edwards, John Wesley and Billy Sunday, William Booth, and of course, Billy Graham, just to name a few. Many waves of revival have swept our country. God is merciful to send many Jonahs to give us the opportunity to fast, pray and repent, but how long will He wait? When will a Nahum rise up and prophesy the swift judgment of an angry God on America?

We are living in important days and in important times. This book contains multiple testimonies of people who have received tremendous personal reward and blessing over just a few years because they teamed up with one church, one ministry here in America that corporately fasts and prays. Thankfully, churches across this country are coming to understand the importance of fasting and humbling ourselves before God.

HE HEARD DANIEL ON THE VERY FIRST DAY!

We can humble ourselves and pray, and seek His face, and expect Him to hear from Heaven and heal our land. He heard Daniel on the very first day!

YOM KIPPUR

Yom Kippur is perhaps the most celebrated holy day on the Jewish calendar. Meaning "Day of Atonement," it was established by God for Israel in Leviticus 16:29-30:

"This shall be a statute forever for you: In the seventh month, on the tenth day of the month, you shall afflict your souls, and do no work at all, whether a native of your own country or a stranger who dwells among you. For on that day the priest shall make atonement for you, to cleanse you, that you may be clean

from all your sins before the LORD."

Notice again the word afflict which means fasting. Even Jews who typically do not observe any other Jewish festival will often participate in Yom Kippur by fasting, attending synagogue and refraining from work to atone for sins against God. Yom Kippur, or the Day of Atonement, is the final day of "appeal" to God for atonement which is preceded by ten Days of Awe that are spent in reflection on one's life and sins.

It was on Yom Kippur in 1963 that the nations of Egypt, Jordan and Syria allied to attack Israel and wipe out that nation. All of Israel had been fasting and repenting of sin before God for 24 hours. The allied enemies of Israel picked the wrong day to attack.

History records that the soldiers literally ran out of the synagogues to the front lines, having had nothing to eat for 24 hours. At first the battle was going toward the Arab armies who pushed Israel back for three days. It appeared that victory for Israel was impossible, but the battle turned on the third day. Even though they were significantly outnumbered Israel's army was victorious and took back what ground they lost, plus even more. Today, when you hear news reports about things happening in the "Occupied Territories," remember that those are the additional lands Israel claimed in the Yom Kippur War. The enemy thinks you are weaker when you fast. He will try to convince you that you are dying without food—but you are not. God is preparing to breathe life into your situation to open a door to His promises.

CONTINUAL PRAYER

Fasting is not a means to promote yourself. The greatest thing fasting will do for you will be to break down all of the stuff that accumulates from this world that blocks you from clear communion with the Father.

As I wrote in my first book, *Fasting: The Private Discipline That Brings Public Reward*, when you are on a prolonged fast, you are praying continually. What I mean is, you have times to get away and pray, whether you feel like it or not. Fasting in and of itself is a continual prayer to God. You are praying 24 hours a day when you are fasting. If you have been fasting all day, you've been praying all day.

Some of the greatest miracles, breakthroughs and seasons of prayer I have ever experienced did not come when I was "feeling led" to pray and fast. They actually came when the last thing I wanted to do was drag myself to my prayer place, but I did and God honored my faithfulness. Jesus said, "*When you pray...When you fast...When you give...*" (see Matthew 6). He expects those who follow Him to do these things whether feeling a special *leading* or not. These things should be part of every believer's life.

There are different levels of fasts. When I first started, I didn't start with 21 days. I just did three days and then I built up to seven days and then 21 days. What I have done recently is a total fast for seven days in January, and then a total fast for three days each month from February to December. That is a total of forty days over the course of a year.

As you fast, target your unsaved loved ones in prayer. Create a "hit list" of people you want to see saved. It is good to be very specific in your prayers during a fast. What is the one most critical thing you want God to do in your life? God told Habakkuk to "write the vision and make it plain" (see Habakkuk 2:2). I dare you to write down the names of those you want to see saved, and when you fast and pray, call those names out to God. As we have seen evidenced here at Free Chapel, I believe you, too, will see breakthrough like you never dreamed!

KEEP YOUR ARMOR FITTING AND YOUR BLADE SHARP!

If you let it, your flesh will take over and rule your life. That is why times of fasting are so crucial to your walk with

God. Fasting helps you establish dominion and authority over your flesh. *"Do not be deceived, God is not mocked; for whatever a man sows, that he will also reap. For he who sows to his flesh will of the flesh reap corruption, but he who sows to the Spirit will of the Spirit reap everlasting life. And let us not grow weary while doing good, for in due season we shall reap if we do not lose heart"* (Galatians 6:7-9 NKJV). Keep your armor fit and your blade sharp!

CHAPTER 7

SEEN BUT NOT HEARD

...If My people who are called by My name will humble themselves, and pray and seek My face, and turn from their wicked ways, then I will hear from heaven, and will forgive their sin and heal their land. Now My eyes will be open and My ears attentive to prayer made in this place.
—[2 Chronicles 7:14-15 NKJV]

I s it possible to fast and the Lord not hear your plea? God said of Israel, *"You cannot fast as you do today and expect your voice to be heard on high"* (Isaiah 58:4 AMP). What were they doing wrong?

Israel was unrepentant and had forsaken the ordinances of God. Though they appeared to be seeking God and delighting in His ways, their sin was all God could see. Instead of truly humbling themselves before God, fasting had become just another faithless mechanical performance full of strife, anger and lashing out.

Though you do not fast to be cleansed of sin (the blood of Jesus is the only solution for sin), you should enter a fast seriously, having repented of any known sins. Fasting will even bring hidden things to the surface so you can repent. As David said, *"Who may ascend into the hill of the LORD? Or who may stand in His holy place? He who has clean hands and a pure heart, who has not lifted up his soul to an idol, nor sworn deceitfully"* (Psalm 24:3-4 NIV).

YOU SHOULD ENTER A FAST, HAVING REPENTED OF ANY KNOWN SINS.

When you fast, your appearance should be normal and you should not draw attention to your "affliction" of fasting through your actions, your treatment of others or your temperament. Though your focus should be on your own needs, the needs of others should be on your heart as well. God said,

> *"Is this not the fast that I have chosen:*
> *To loose the bonds of wickedness,*
> *To undo the heavy burdens,*
> *To let the oppressed go free,*
> *And that you break every yoke?*
> *Is it not to share your bread with the hungry,*
> *And that you bring to your house the poor who are cast out;*
> *When you see the naked, that you cover him,*
> *And not hide yourself from your own flesh?"*
> (Isaiah 58:6-7 NKJV)

The Israelites questioned why they fasted with no answer from God. The Lord called Isaiah to *"cry aloud and spare not,"* telling the people to repent of their transgressions, to fast the way God ordained and also, to tell them what would happen when they do...

> *"Then your light shall break forth like the morning,*
> *Your healing shall spring forth speedily,*

> *And your righteousness shall go before you;*
> *The glory of the LORD shall be your rear guard.*
> *Then you shall call, and the LORD will answer;*
> *You shall cry, and He will say, 'Here I am.'"*
> (Isaiah 58:8-9 NKJV)

SHINING LIGHT

What does *"your light shall break forth like the morning"* mean? Illumination. Jesus said, *"You are the light of the world. A city on a hill cannot be hidden"* (Matthew 5:14 NIV). God intended Israel to be a "light" in darkness to other nations, glorifying the God of Creation by their actions and by the blessings of God apparent on their lives, thus drawing others to God. Likewise, in our lives as children of God, our light will break forth and be apparent to others—I imagine much like the glow on the face of Moses when he descended the mountain after spending time with God. I really believe that God has brought illumination to my life and to my ministry, for which I can take no credit. Our TV ministry is reaching farther than ever. A viewer wrote recently that she had gone on a 40-day fast from meat using my first book and workbook on fasting. She said:

> *"I had never completed a fast of this length, but using the book*

*really helped me to remain steadfast. I heard God clearer than I've
ever heard Him and my life will never be the same. Thank you
for the opportunity to partner with you and your ministry. God is
truly using you in a powerful way to minister to His people and
to the lost."*

HEALTH SPRINGS FORTH

I have to let these testimonies explain this point. My friend,
Bob Rogers, is a Pastor in Kentucky. He has been on sixteen 21-
day fasts and I believe six 40-day fasts. This testimony is about
a man in his church who had lost his bridgework (teeth) and
couldn't find them anywhere, so he had a new bridge made
and joined in the first of the year fast.

Somewhere around the fourteenth day of their fast, the
man began to cough pretty severely. In fact, he got into such
a coughing fit, that he coughed up something solid—his
original bridgework! This is a true story! Apparently they had
come loose in the night and he had somehow aspirated them
into his lung. (He must be a *really* deep sleeper!) It's one thing
to be sick and be healed speedily. It is another for God to heal
you of an issue before it makes you sick. Had that foreign
object stayed in his lung much longer, he would have become
very ill and required major surgery to have it removed.

A woman emailed this awesome testimony. She had been plagued for a few years with protruding "knots" at the base of her spine. You could place your hand on her back and feel them very easily. They caused her severe, sometimes debilitating pain. She and her husband were part of our 21-day fast at the beginning of the year. The first three days they went on a total fast, drinking only water, and then a Daniel fast for the remaining 18 days. On the second day, her back was hurting badly with no relief. She went over her prayer list—calling out the names of unsaved family members and other needs, and asking the Lord to please heal her back. On the third day...she was praying over her list and asking the Lord again to heal the knots. She placed her hand on them to "lay hands on herself," only to find that they were no longer there! She had been completely healed on just the second day of her fast and had not even realized it!

This letter also attests to health springing forth speedily from fasting:

"Our son is nineteen-years old, and was diagnosed with Cystic Fibrosis at the age of five. Recently, he was admitted to the hospital because his oxygen level had fallen to 70%. About a week after the fast ended, he turned critical, and I was notified that his lungs could fail at any moment. I immediately called my husband,

spiritual friends and my family. I called a solemn assembly of prayer and fasting for twenty-four hours, beginning at 5:00 p.m. that Thursday until 5:00 p.m. Friday. Needless to say at 4:00 p.m. Friday, the twenty-third hour of the fast, my son's carbon dioxide test came back normal! What a miracle. Only God could do this. There was nothing the medical doctor could do. God is faithful. I'm so thankful for my Church at Free Chapel and their obedience to obey God in prayer and fasting. My husband, my twenty-one year old son and I have been involved in this twenty-one day fast and am thankful it was going on during this time."

RIGHTEOUSNESS

The Lord says that when you fast, "Your righteousness shall go before you."

Your faith, your right standing with God will cause you to move into areas that you would not have moved if you had not fasted. Doors will open to you that were not opened before, and your influence will go out like ripples in a pond. One woman wrote: "I joined two friends in a 21 day fast, after which the Holy Spirit delivered to me a special message about fasting. At His prodding I typed out the message and have shared it with others. Praise the Lord—the message touched hearts and helped others to understand the power of fasting. It is exciting to *hear what God is doing in their lives because of their faithfulness to fast."*

When my brother and I started our first revival meetings we took turns fasting. I would fast on the days he preached and he would fast the days I preached. We knew we had the right intentions in mind, but we were a little surprised when that two or three day revival lasted several weeks. We looked like half-starved refugees when the revival ended, but we had tapped into something powerful. I believe the doors that have been opened to me have been a direct result of His promises being fulfilled because of fasting. There are people whose lives can be forever made better because of your righteousness going forth with influence.

REARGUARD

Most of us have heard the slang expression: "I've got your back." It means that someone you trust is watching out for anything that may try to sneak up behind you and bring you harm. When you fast, Isaiah said, *"The God of Israel will be your rear guard"* (Isaiah 52:12 NKJV).

Further, God says, *"No weapon formed against you shall prosper, and every tongue which rises against you in judgment you shall condemn. This is the heritage of the servants of the LORD,* and their righteousness is from Me" (Isaiah 54:17 NKJV). No wonder the devil wants fasting to remain the best-kept secret in the kingdom.

HE WILL HEAR AND ANSWER

The Israelites were fasting, but with wrong motives. They could not find God, but when we fast according to His plan, He says, *"Then you shall call, and the LORD will answer; You shall cry, and He will say, 'Here I am'"* (Isaiah 58:9 NKJV). Remember what the angel told Daniel in Daniel chapter 10? From the first day that Daniel began to fast, God heard. The only thing that held up his answer was battle in the heavenlies!

> FROM THE FIRST DAY THAT DANIEL BEGAN TO FAST, GOD HEARD.

A woman who volunteers for Free Chapel gave the most amazing testimony to this fact. Her parents had been in severe financial trouble for over a year. They had been given notice of foreclosure proceedings if they did not pay $5500. She called her unsaved brothers and asked them if they wanted to join her in doing something that would help her parents in this desperate situation. God backed her up! Her brothers agreed and they began to fast.

Within 15 days of the house being foreclosed, her parents received a phone call. Her father had applied for disability in 2000, but it took six years for them to get around to having the hearing on his case. They called to inform the family that his disability application had been approved and a check was in the mail that very day in the amount of—are you ready for this?—$86,000, which included the back pay from 2000. In addition, he would be getting disability payments monthly. There is no way her brothers can deny that God is the one who brought about this miracle.

God's promises don't stop there. He also says,

"...Then shall thy light rise in obscurity, and thy darkness be as the noon day: And the LORD shall guide thee continually, and satisfy thy soul in drought, and make fat thy bones: and thou shalt be like a watered garden, and like a spring of water, whose waters fail not. And they that shall be of thee shall build the old waste places: thou shalt raise up the foundations of many generations" (Isaiah 58:10-12).

OBSCURITY AND DARKNESS

"Your light will rise out of obscurity..." In other words, in situations you face that are just overwhelming and you don't know how to find your way through the darkness of obscurity

and confusion, God will cause your light to shine on the path you are to take.

My friend, Pastor Bob Rogers, had another wonderful testimony come forth out of his congregation. They go on a corporate fast each year just like we do here at Free Chapel. There was a man who lost his bakery business. Hard times hit and the business went under just before the Christmas season. All he could afford to give his wife that year for Christmas was a seventy-five cent card. In January, he joined the 21-day fast.

At the end of the fast, he had an appointment to see his accountant in order to prepare his taxes and review the losses of the previous year. Now remember—he had fasted and sought God. When he arrived at the office, his accountant said, "I've been trying to call you, but your number has been disconnected. I heard about a man in Louisville who owns four bakeries. He wants to sell the businesses and I thought about you. He wants to sell them for just $25,000."

The man just kind of smirked and said, "I can't even afford to pay a $25 light bill right now. How can I come up with that kind of cash?" Still discouraged, the man left. On the way home he had stopped at a "stop" sign. The white letters on the red background seemed more vivid than usual. While he was stopped, he sensed the Holy Spirit saying, "For 21 days you have asked me to bless you, did you not? Turn back."

He immediately turned his car around and went back to ask for the name and number of the man selling the bakeries. Three men from his church gave him the money upfront and he was able to pay them back in full within six months. He could barely afford a card for his wife the Christmas before. At the end of their first year of giving their first days of the year to the Lord in fasting and prayer, he and his wife were so prosperous that she gave him an airplane for Christmas that year!

The Lord guided him back to his promise. That is another benefit of fasting: The Lord will guide you continually. Though the path before you may be obscure, when you fast and pray in faith, God will reward you and guide you. *"Your ears shall hear a word behind you, saying, 'This is the way, walk in it'"* (Isaiah 30:21 NKJV).

> YOU WILL RAISE UP A FOUNDATION FOR MANY GENERATIONS.

RAISE A FOUNDATION

Finally, and this is very close to my heart, when you fast, "You will raise up a foundation for many generations."

When you fast, you begin to lay a spiritual foundation that not only affects your life, but God says you will also affect the generations to come after you. I don't just fast for myself, I fast for my children, my future grandchildren and so on. I have laid a foundation through my devotion to God that He will build upon because He found an inroad to my family. A woman who watches the Kingdom Connection broadcast on TBN wrote to share a remarkable testimony to this effect.

"I did my first 21-day fast after seeing Pastor Franklin's teaching. I believe the Lord told me I would be fasting for my sick father, who was not yet a believer. I felt I had a promise from God that my Dad would not leave this earth without my knowing he is saved. Nearly 3 months after the fast, my daddy died. But as the Lord promised, three days before his death he assured me that he had asked Jesus into his heart!

I also fasted for my 22-year-old prodigal daughter, who walked away from the Lord when she was 18. I began this year with the 21-day Daniel fast, again with my daughter as my focus. I recently heard from my daughter. She wanted to tell me that she is coming to church on Easter Sunday! It will be the first time in four and one-half years. The Lord confirmed that this has occurred as a result of my fast. I am making fasting a discipline in my life."

Fasting can end the demonic attack on your family.

Fasting can break the generational curses. When you fast, you lay a new foundation of blessing that will be transferred over to your children and your children's children. For this reason alone I believe the head of any family who has ever been touched by divorce, abuse, molestation, etc.—you should designate a fast for your family and children in order to bind those demonic attachments from your generations. *"And you shall be called the Repairer of the Breach, The Restorer of Streets to Dwell In"* (Isaiah 58:12b NKJV).

CHAPTER 8

GO FOR IT

Therefore, brethren, be even more diligent to

make your call and election sure, for if you do

these things you will never stumble; for so an

entrance will be supplied to you abundantly

into the everlasting kingdom of our

Lord and Savior Jesus Christ.

—[2 Peter 1:10-11 NKJV]

When the Israelites left Egypt, God had provided manna for them daily, as well as clothing and shoes that did not wear out. Idolatry and unfaithfulness had entered the hearts of the older generation and they were left to wander in the wilderness for 40 years. There was an entire generation that had grown up in the wilderness, listening to stories of the wonders that God had done to deliver Israel from Egyptian slavery—the plagues, the miracles, the plundering, the parting of the Red Sea, the drowning of Pharaoh's army, the fire by night and cloud by day, and the Ten Commandments written in stone. For nearly forty years they had eaten manna in the morning and manna in the evening, while wondering about a land flowing with mild and honey (Joshua 5:5)

Moses had been laid to rest. Joshua was now in charge—things were changing. The command came from Joshua: *"Sanctify yourselves, for tomorrow the LORD will do wonders among you"* (Joshua 3:5 NKJV). There must have been an extreme excitement spreading throughout the camp, but the Lord would do wonders only "if" the children of Israel would sanctify themselves.

The Hebrew root for "sanctify" is *"qadhash"* which is also the root for "holy." God said: *"I am the Lord your God; consecrate yourselves and be holy, because I am holy"* (Leviticus 11:44 NIV).

Sanctification is the process of becoming holy in daily life; it is practicing purity and being set apart from the world and from sin. Sanctification is allowing the Holy Spirit to make

FASTING IS AN EXCELLENT MEANS OF SANCTIFYING YOURSELF.

us more like Jesus in what we do, in what we think and in what we desire. We do not hear much about sanctification from the pulpits these days, but if we are to see God do wonders in our midst, we must confront sin in our lives and live holy.

God was about to lead His chosen people out against the enemies of God, but they could not stand if they were not holy. This is clearly seen in the contrast between Israel's supernatural victory against the city of Jericho (Joshua chapter 6), and their defeat in Joshua chapter 7 by the tiny army of Ai after Israel had sinned by having stolen things in their midst.

KNOWING GOD'S WILL

We desire to be in the Will of God and to walk according to His plans. Sanctification is the key to being in God's will. As Paul said, *"For this is the will of God, even your sanctification"* (1 Thessalonians 4:3). There is no need to try to find some mysterious "wheel of God" out there. You cannot follow

God's leading until you start where Paul said start.

"It is God's will that you should be sanctified: that you should avoid sexual immorality; that each of you should learn to control his own body in a way that is holy and honorable, not in passionate lust like the heathen, who do not know God; and that in this matter no one should wrong his brother or take advantage of him. The Lord will punish men for all such sins, as we have already told you and warned you. For God did not call us to be impure, but to live a holy life. Therefore, he who rejects this instruction does not reject man but God, who gives you his Holy Spirit." (1 Thessalonians 4:3-8 NIV)

FASTING WILL HELP YOU IDENTIFY AREAS OF HIDDEN SIN IN YOUR LIFE.

Fasting is an essential means of sanctifying yourself, pulling yourself away from the world and getting closer to God. Fasting allows you to filter your life and to set yourself apart to seek the Lord. Jesus prayed for us...

"They are not of the world, just as I am not of the world. Sanctify them by Your truth. Your word is truth. As You sent Me into the world, I also have sent them into the world. And for their sakes I sanctify Myself, that they also may be sanctified by the truth." (John 17:16-19 NKJV)

As I've stated in previous chapters, fasting will help

you identify areas of even hidden sin and things that are displeasing to God in your life. Fasting helps you discern between serving the flesh and serving the spirit. *"For if the blood of bulls and goats and the ashes of a heifer, sprinkling the unclean, sanctifies for the purifying of the flesh, how much more shall the blood of Christ, who through the eternal Spirit offered Himself without spot to God, cleanse your conscience from dead works to serve the living God?"* (Hebrews 9:13-14 NKJV). If we are in Christ, His blood cleanses us from dead works, enabling us to serve God in Holiness.

NECESSITY OF SANCTIFICATION

Why do we need to sanctify ourselves? We have no place in our heart for pride. We have no place in our heart for complacency. If God has blessed your life, you are critically in need of sanctifying yourself. Beware of being a member of the first church of the "frozen chosen." Do not let the blessings of the past interfere with the blessings of the future. The blessings of the future will be greater than anything He has done in the past.

David was a man after God's heart, yet he cried out, *"Create in me a clean heart, O God; and renew a right spirit within me"* (Psalm 51:10). We need a sanctification of *motives*.

We need a sanctification of *desires*. We need a sanctification of *attitudes*. We need a sanctification of the *right spirit*. We need a sanctification of our *flesh*.

RESPONSIBILITY OF SANCTIFICATION

The writer of the book of Hebrews warns: *"Beware, brethren, lest there be in any of you an evil heart of unbelief in departing from the living God; but exhort one another daily, while it is called 'Today,' lest any of you be hardened through the deceitfulness of sin"* (Hebrews 3:12-13 NKJV). While the leadership should certainly set an example in personal sanctification and holy living, it is the responsibility of every believer to "exhort" fellow believers. "Exhort" means to be abrasive with one another...to encourage one another... to push one another to live holy so that no one falls into temptation and ends up turning away from God.

CROSSING OVER

Joshua gave orders for the officers to command the people saying

"When you see the ark of the covenant of the LORD your God, and the priests, the Levites, bearing it, then you shall set out from your place and go after it. Yet there shall be a space between

you and it, about two thousand cubits by measure. Do not come near it, that you may know the way by which you must go, for you have not passed this way before." (Joshua 3:3-4 NKJV)

They were to "stand back and watch God!" They were about to see the wonders they had heard about, but never seen for themselves. As soon as the soles of their feet touched the water of the overflowing Jordan River, the waters separated as they had in the Red Sea, allowing the new generation to pass through the waters on dry ground. *"Then the priests who bore the ark of the covenant of the LORD stood firm on dry ground in the midst of the Jordan; and all Israel crossed over on dry ground, until all the people had crossed completely over the Jordan"* (Joshua 3:17 NKJV).

WHEN YOU SANCTIFY YOURSELF UNTO GOD, IT MOVES YOU OFF THE BANK AND INTO THE MIRACLES!

When you fast and sanctify yourself unto God, it moves you off the bank and into the miracles! There are too many people on the edges of what God is doing, and not enough of us standing firmly in the middle of His will. Do you want things to change in your home? You are the priest of your home—fast, sanctify yourself and take a firm stand in the middle of God's will! When your family sees you stepping off of the edge of mere "Sunday morning religion" and getting right into the middle of what God is doing—they will follow and find God's direction for their lives.

I want you to notice that the children of Israel all crossed at the same place. You should be attached to a local body of believers instead of just trying to find your own way. If ever there was a time where we needed to be crossing together, taking a firm, united stand against sin in this nation, it is now. We need each other. We need a spirit of togetherness. We need a spirit of trust. We need a spirit of unity. We need a spirit of compassion one for another.

BLESSING OF SANCTIFICATION

Joshua's words went out to "the chosen generation." God had waited until all those who were stiff-necked and rebellious had grown old and died. That younger generation would go forth and inherit the promises. After they crossed the Jordan, God told Joshua to *"make flint knives for yourself, and circumcise the sons of Israel again the second time"* (Joshua 5:2 NKJV). The older generation was circumcised, but the younger generation had not been. They were to bear the mark of Covenant in their flesh before God would take them any further.

Circumcision speaks of sanctification of the flesh. It is

cutting away dead things and hidden sins. You can look good publicly, raising your hands, giving your offerings, praying and even fasting; but all the while hiding deadly sins. You are sanctified by the Blood of Jesus when you first accept Him as your Lord and Savior, but over time, complacency and hidden sins can creep into your heart. You can just start drifting and you let your standard down. Paul explained this clearly to the Galatians:

"Now the works of the flesh are evident, which are: adultery, fornication, uncleanness, lewdness, idolatry, sorcery, hatred, contentions, jealousies, outbursts of wrath, selfish ambitions, dissensions, heresies, envy, murders, drunkenness, revelries, and the like; of which I tell you beforehand, just as I also told you in time past, that those who practice such things will not inherit the kingdom of God." (Galatians 5:19-21 NKJV)

The blessing of sanctification brings with it the promises of God's covenant and life in the Spirit..."*The fruit of the Spirit is love, joy, peace, longsuffering, kindness, goodness, faithfulness, gentleness, self-control. Against such there is no law. And those who are Christ's have crucified the flesh with its passions and desires. If we live in the Spirit, let us also walk in the Spirit. Let us not become conceited, provoking one another, envying one another"* (Galatians 5:22-26 NKJV).

Fasting sharpens the blade...sharpens the Word in your heart and in your mouth, allowing you to cut away the dead flesh and hidden sin, as you set yourself apart for God.

What is Your "It"?

Over twenty years ago when the Lord first called me to preach, He showed me some things that were for a time and season yet to come. I could not walk into all of His promise at once, but I knew He would lead me in His Will as I was willing to sanctify myself and follow him. Recently, the Lord has stirred my spirit with a sense that now is the time. It is as if He is saying, "You've prayed about it. You've dreamed about it. You've asked me for it. You've longed for it. It's been prophesied over you...prepare yourself."

I traveled back to North Carolina, where I was born and raised. My grandfather still has a home in Middlesex, North Carolina. It is a beautiful mansion-like homestead set on acres of rolling, lush farmland with horses, cattle, even his own private airstrip for his plane. Twenty-eight children were raised in that house over the years, and all of them serve the Lord.

During that special visit back to my roots, my heritage, I spent time each day walking that airstrip and the fields in prayer and communion with God. I felt the Holy Spirit's leading to visit the place down the road where He first called me to preach. I had not been back there in twenty-two years. I went down to that wonderful old Church of God sanctuary and sat down in the very spot of my calling. I can remember like it was yesterday. I was on a three-day fast and I was crying out, "Oh, God, can You use me? Why are You calling me to preach? I can't do it. I don't know how to preach. I'm afraid. I'm not worthy. I'm not good enough." I was giving Him all the excuses and all the fear. I didn't realize that during that three-day fast I was cutting off the flesh with a sharp knife.

Finally, on the third day, I heard His voice in my spirit say, "I've called you to preach. Go and do what I've called you to do." I said, "Lord, if this is truly Your will, then let my mother confirm it when I get home, even though it's past midnight. Let her be up and let her confirm it." I was young, and it never hurts to ask for clarity! I walked out of that tiny sanctuary weeping, got into my car and drove barely a quarter mile home. When I walked back to Mom's bedroom, she was on her knees praying. As soon as I saw her, she whirled around, pointed her finger and started speaking with stammering lips: "Jentezen, God has called you to preach. Go and do what He has called you to do."

Sitting in that very same spot, more than twenty years later, I was absolutely overwhelmed. Emotions like I have never felt before in my life washed over me. It was in that moment that I again sensed the leading of the Spirit in my heart directing me to fast and sanctify myself a second time because He had prophetically led me back to that spot where I started. He was about to begin a brand new thing in my life. Like the children of Israel, it was as if He said, "You've never been this way before."

WHAT ABOUT YOU?

What if you set yourself to diligently seek the Lord, sanctifying yourself with a fast and journey back to the spot where it all began...where He saved you, set you free, filled you with His Spirit and called you out? I actually physically traveled to that spot, but if you cannot do that, you can go back mentally. You can recall the ancient landmark, that same simplicity, innocence and dedication with which you first responded to His voice.

GOD WANTS YOU TO ASK HIM FOR THINGS THAT ARE BIGGER THAN YOURSELF!

God wants you to ask Him for—believe Him for—things

that are bigger than yourself. I am now over forty years old, but I cannot just float through life. I can't kick back and wait for retirement. I have too much promised! I want to reap the harvest. The children of Israel had made it through the wilderness. They had stopped eating manna and had begun to eat the good fruit of the land. They lived along a river and they could have easily set-up trade with those from the big city of Jericho, but that was not their destiny.

Fasting will bring you into destiny. Fasting will bring you into alignment with God's plan for your life. Just as Joshua called the children of promise to sanctify themselves—I beleive that likewise, your "tomorrow" is just around the corner. God is going to do wonders in your life, leading you places you have never been before. Now is the time to fast, to seek God diligently to sanctify yourself, to discern God's priorities and to walk in His promises. *Go for it!*

Notes

_____

_____

_____

_____

_____

_____

_____

_____

_____

_____

_____

NOTES

_____

_____

_____

_____

_____

_____

_____

_____

_____

notes

_____

_____

_____

_____

_____

_____

_____

_____

_____

_____

notes

_____

_____

_____

_____

_____

_____

_____

_____

_____

_____

_____

notes

_____

_____

_____

_____

_____

_____

_____

_____

_____

_____

NOTES

_____

_____

_____

_____

_____

_____

_____

_____

_____

_____

NOTES

_____

_____

_____

_____

_____

_____

_____

_____

_____

ABOUT THE AUTHOR

As a pastor, teacher and author, Jentezen Franklin pursues a dream of helping people encounter God through inspired worship and relevant application of God's Word.

Through Jentezen Franklin Ministries, he is impacting generations through varied worldwide outreaches and the life-changing television broadcast, Kingdom Connection. He is also the Senior Pastor of Free Chapel in Gainesville, Georgia. Jentezen Franklin and his wife, Cherise, have five children.

FOR MORE INFORMATION WRITE TO:

JENTEZEN FRANKLIN MINISTRIES
P.O. BOX 315
GAINESVILLE, GA 30503

OR VISIT US ON THE WEB:

www.jentezenfranklin.org
www.freechapel.org